BRISTOL ON OLD POSTCARDS

Volume Two

Compiled by

Janet and Derek Fisher
Mildred and Francis Ford
(founder members of Bristol Postcard Club)

1. The Broad Quay, Bristol. A photograph taken from the top deck of a tram, about 1908. The newly-built C.W.S. building features prominently in the centre of the picture. Close by is the Dublin shed, where the ships from Ireland unloaded. This postcard, published by Harvey Barton and Son Ltd., Bristol, was postally used in 1911.

£3.95

2. Political parties and candidates made extensive use of postcards in promoting their ideas and as election propaganda. This superb example comes from 1905. Sir Thomas Joseph Lennard lived at Henbury Hill House, near Bristol, and was Liberal M.P. from 1904 until he retired in 1921.

**Designed and Published by
Reflections of a Bygone Age,
Keyworth, Nottingham
1985**

**Printed by
Adlard Print and Typesetting Services,
Ruddington, Notts.**

ISBN 0 946245 10 X

Acknowledgements:

The compilers would like to thank Andrew Palmer, for the loan of illus. 118; Geoff Rose, for information on illus. 117; Ted Houghton, who helped with proof-reading.

INDEX

Advertisement cards	155-165
Aerial views	169-171
Albion Dockyard	38
All Saints Lane	19
Ashley Down	99-101
Ashton	45-46
Avonmouth	60-62
Baldwin Street	168
Bedminster	105-107, 137
Belgrave Road	113
Bishopston	93-98
Bishopsworth	66-68
Blackboy Hill	112, 116, 144
Brick Street	50
Bridge Street	15
Brislington	72-74
Broad Quay	1
Broad Weir	65
Characters	146-148
Cheltenham Road	40
City Docks	36-37
Clare Street	149, 168
Clifton	9, 63, 108-110
Clifton Bridge	47, 136
Coldharbour Road	41
Coliseum	30-31
Colston Street	29
Comic cards	174-179
Corn Street	18, 173
Coronation Road	35
Dolphin Street	16
Downend	90-92
Eastville	86
Fire Brigade	120-122
Fishponds	81-83
Football cards	123-124
Frenchay	87
Frogmore Street	167
General Hospital	27-28
Hanham	78-80
Henbury	51-52
Heraldic card	4
High Street	145
Horfield	102-104

Horsefair	25
Hotwells	42-44
King Street	166
Kingswood	126, 172
Maps	3, 5
Marlborough Street	150
Merchant Street	21
Milk Street	22
Narrow Wine Street	17
Newfoundland Road	23
Norman Tower	10
Novelty cards	174-175
Old Market Street	49
Park Street	12, 14, 141
Political card	2
Pottery theme	160-161
Queens Road	32
Queen Square	170
Railway stations	131-139, 151, 169
Redcliffe Hill	171
Royal visits	149-151
Rupert Street	24
St. Anne's	75-77, 139
St. Augustine's Bridge	7
St. Augustine's Church	6, 11
St. Michaels Hill	64
St. Raphaels	33
Schools	39, 125-130
Sea Mills	54-56
Shirehampton	57-59
Shop Fronts	140-145
Stapleton	88-89
Stapleton Road	84-85
Stokes Croft	26, 142
Tower Hill	48
Trams	114-119
University	13
Vauxhall Bridge	34
Wells Road	69-71
Westbury-on-Trym	53
Whiteladies Road	111, 143
Wine Street	20, 140
Zoo	152-154

INTRODUCTION

Picture Postcards were not introduced in Britain until 1894, though they had been popular on the Continent for over 20 years. The early British cards were known as Court Cards (size 115 x 89 mm), smaller than the Continental size of 140 x 89 mm, and the message had to be written on the same side as the picture, leaving the back for the stamp and address. This obviously inhibited the possibilities for illustrations, so when the Post Office permitted the use of the larger-size card (1899) and the 'divided back' (1902) where message and address occupied the same side, the publishers were able to exploit the postcard much more effectively, and a flood of cards on every imaginable subject was produced.

The postcard fulfilled several functions: it was a medium for communicating simple messages and greetings (mail was reliably delivered within 24 hours, and over short distances, on the same day). Firms used them as advertising material and correspondence cards. Photographs of special events and disasters provided a unique pictorial record of local happenings. Comic postcards gave people the opportunity to send risqué messages to their friends. Soon, the collecting of all these cards became a major hobby, and the reign of Edward VII paralleled the 'golden age' of Picture Postcards, with many thousands of families amassing vast numbers sent from all over Britain (and, for those with wealthy connections, the Continent). Specialist magazines catered for the craze, and publishers produced cards on all kinds of themes: railways, actresses, military, shipping, glamour, children, heraldic, royalty, political - as well as greetings, comic cards and street scenes. The Great War saw new themes developed - patriotic, political satire, and beautiful silk cards, embroidered in France, and sent home by British tommies to be lovingly treasured. Postcard collecting ceased to have the same meaning and appeal after the war, though. The quality of production deteriorated (some of the best pre-1914 cards had been printed in Germany), the postage rate doubled, and the national mood and social conditions had changed out of all recognition: it was a new era, with changed values and priorities. 'Golden Age' postcards lay neglected in their albums in attics for years, until a few enthusiasts in the 1950's ushered a new-found appreciation for the beautiful old cards to a whole new generation. Their availability, though, remained confined to the shelves of occasional book and antique shops, and new-wave collectors didn't find it easy to build up collections. All that changed in the 1970's. A travelling exhibition organised by the Victoria and Albert Museum, the emergence of specialist dealers, magazines, catalogues and fairs, had the effect of encouraging a host of new collectors and a consequent upsurge in prices. By then, Edwardian albums were emerging from the attics, as their original owners or their sons and daughters died. Now, the hobby is thriving, and the beautiful postcard issues of the Edwardian era are once again lovingly collected.

The second volume of **BRISTOL ON OLD POSTCARDS** features another superb selection of cards. Response to the first book, published in 1983, has been tremendous, and we're sure readers will enjoy this further choice. In order to do justice to some of the beautiful artist-drawn and advertising postcards, this book includes several pages in full colour. In fact, most of the cards illustrated were originally published in black and white, some on printing machines, some by a photographic process. It is these latter types showing Edwardian street scenes that are currently most in demand from contemporary collectors. The most favoured - and valuable - ones are those produced in small quantities by local photographers. Often, only a few examples of each have survived, and today can be worth many pounds.

It's worth remembering, though, that of all the billions of postcards published since 1894, only a small fraction are worth more than a few pence. Most greetings, views, comics and thematics still exist in huge quantities and can be bought cheaply. The illustrations in this book represent some of the more unusual Bristol postcards and a large proportion of them have not appeared in book form before.

One of the fascinations of postcard collecting is that you're never quite sure what cards will turn up next. Checklists of issues by local photographers like Garratt can only be compiled on the basis of what has so far been discovered - but new cards are constantly being discovered. Another appeal of the hobby is the fact that used postcards often include interesting messages and/or postmark. Although the collecting of picture postcards has become a major hobby in Great Britain, there is still a great deal of research to be done.

Several specialist postcard fairs are held regularly in and around Bristol. It is worth keeping an eye on the local press for advance announcements and advertisements.

The cards chosen for this book represent only a fraction of those available featuring Bristol and its environs, but hopefully they will give readers a flavour of life in the Edwardian city - and of the riches waiting on old picture postcards.

THE COMPILERS

Janet Fisher's enthusiasm for picture postcards was kindled as a child when she was allowed to look through her grandmother's collection of cards of the Queen's dolls house: her serious collecting began about six years ago, aided and abetted by Derek, and her first purchases were of cards of Weston-super-Mare. The lovely fashions of the early 1900's portrayed on the postcards really caught her imagination. During this time Janet's interest in the seaside resort wavered in favour of 'Old Bristol', and she has now amassed a considerable collection. Derek is also keen on stamp collecting and photography.

Mildred Ford was lucky enough to inherit a postcard album that had belonged to her mother. Included in it were about forty First World War silk cards. Through her husband Francis's interest in stamp collecting, and the gradual introduction of postcards to stamp fairs, the inherited collection began to grow. Their favourite artist was A.R. Quinton, with Old Bristol and Great Western Railway Officials vying for equal attention. Mildred's collecting also extends to buttonhooks and crested china, while Francis, apart from his philatelic interest, is keen on model railways and local history.

All four are Bristolians, and met through their shared interests of stamps and postcards; with three friends they became the founder-members of the Bristol Postcard Club in October 1981. Their enthusiasms have played a big part in building up that club, whose most recent success (September 1985) was in winning the BIPEX club competition, complementing the 1983 trophy.

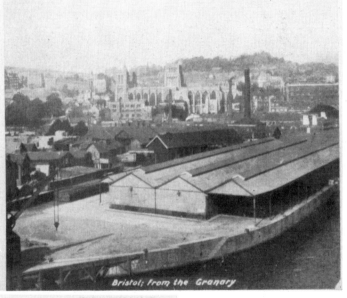

3. John Walker and Co. Ltd., map card no. 152, one of a set of six for Bristol.

4. View of Bristol Cathedral from the Granary, which stood on the site of the present Industrial Museum. The Granary was destroyed in the blitz of January 1941. "Heraldic Series of Postcards", no. 293, by F.S.O.

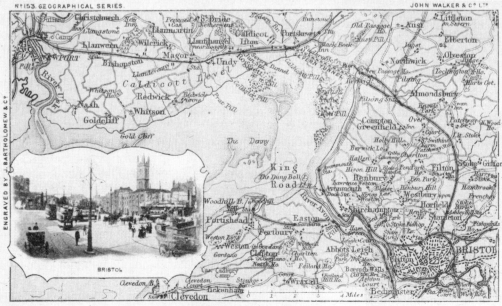

5. Another map card (No. 153) by Walker, but showing the Bristol area in more detail.

St. Augustine's Church & College Green. Bristol. 740.

6. St. Augustine's Church, on a postcard by the York Publishing Co. (No. 740). This lovely old church was founded in 1240, rebuilt in 1480, lengthened in 1780 and eventually restored in the 1870's. However, it became redundant in the 1930's and although only slightly damaged during the war it was demolished in 1962. The Royal Hotel can be seen behind the tower of the church, and the dome of 'E' shed can be seen in the foreground. A much more peaceful scene than that of today.

7. St. Augustine's Bridge and Hippodrome. The Hippodrome was built in 1912, and became the home of Music Hall and Pantomime. On St. Augustine's Parade, visitors could stay at the Drawbridge Hotel for 3/6d bed and breakfast! They could then book a passage on the Canadian Pacific Railway, and purchase portmanteaus for the journey.

St. Augustine's Bridge and Hippodrome, Bristol. 1629.

8. Photographic postcard taken in the late 1920's of two Daimler charabancs. The Cliftonian has the registration no. HT2398. Bringing an elite company to the Hippodrome for an afternoon matinee, perhaps?

9. Early card with views of Clifton; before 1902 the address was the only thing permitted on the non-picture side of the card. Published by J. Baker & Son, Clifton, and printed in Germany. Posted in 1904.

10. 'Oilette' postcard published by Raphael Tuck, no. 6205, *Old Bristol*. The Norman Arch and Tower, before the Central Library was built, situated near the Cathedral. Postally used in 1908.

11. A little artistic licence taken by Evacustes A. Phipson! The painting is dated 1864, but the west towers of the Cathedral were not completed until 1887. Card published by J. Salmon.

12. Park Street. Very peaceful scene, about 1905, with not a motor car in sight! Many of the buildings were damaged or destroyed during the 1939-45 war, and when re-built, the upper storeys were re-built in the same style. Photographic postcard by J.C. Young, Redfield, about 1905.

13. The University Tower nearing completion in 1924. It is sur-rounded by wooden scaffolding, and is one of Bristol's best-known landmarks.

14. Park Street. The opposite view to no. 12, but taken at a later date. Two early motor buses can be seen, plus the inevitable horse and cart! Portrait enlargements cost just 2/3d. A postcard in the "Bee" series by Burgess and Co., Bristol.

15. Bridge Street, on July 8th, 1908, the day Edward VII came with his Queen to open the Royal Edward Dock at Avonmouth. This view is looking from High Street toward Dolphin Street. A few buildings on the right survived the blitz of 1940, only to be demolished later.

16. Dolphin Street, decorated for the same occasion as the previous card. This view is looking from the top of Bridge Street to Union Street. Peter Street is the turning on the right. All the buildings were lost in 1940. Postally used in 1908.

17. Narrow Wine Street, about 1910. This ran from the top of Union Street. Message on the back of the card states:- *Halford Cycle Co. 3, Narrow Wine Street, Bristol, "where Uncle Bert lives"*. Business signs and billboards added so much character to this street, the postcard shop being very prominent! York Publishing Co.

18. Corn Street, looking from the Centre. St. Werburgh's Church was demolished in 1878 for road widening! It was re-erected in Mina Road. George Gibbs, the gunsmith, to the left of the picture, is still trading at Perry Row.

19. All Saints Lane. A Fred Little photograph, looking from Corn Street towards St. Nicholas Church, through the fruit and vegetable market. The building with no. 56 on the wall was the Norwich Union Insurance Co., now Carwardines' tea rooms. Rummer wine vaults and hotel, originally a coaching inn.

20. Wine Street, about 1914, on a postcard photograph by Garratt, looking toward the site of the High Cross. H. Samuel can be seen centre right advertising *"Manchester famous Acme Lever watches, with silver Albert for 25/-, seven year warranty"*! Motor cycle with wicker basket sidecar can be seen right foreground.

21. Merchant Street. A postcard showing the floods of 16th March, 1889. One third of the city was submerged, and recorded as the worst floods since 1809. The view is looking from Fairfax Street towards what is now Debenhams. The Portrait Room signs on the left are approximately where the Post Office now stands. The postcard is taken from a Fred Little photograph.

22. Milk Street. Old King Street is off to the right, looking from Debenhams towards Merchant Street. This watchman's box was built about 1820, and used by night watchmen, before the days of the Police, and was demolished in 1913. "Charlies", patrolled the streets at night and sheltered in these boxes.

23. Newfoundland Road, on a postcard sent in 1916. The gabled building on the right of the picture is St. Agnes school, and the two taller gables were built in 1908. St. Nicholas Road is off to the right in the distance. All the buildings on the left of the picture were demolished for the M.32; not now a place for a leisurely stroll as the ladies in the photograph were! Wonder what thoughts were going through the mind of the little lad in the foreground! Viner's series postcard.

24. Rupert Street, showing Christmas Street leading to St. John's arch, the only city gateway left. The buildings in the centre of the picture were demolished for the erection of Electricity House. Card by E.C. Stevens of Arley Hill, Bristol.

25. The Horsefair, about 1910. St. James's church with tower, and the Welsh Congregational church, can be seen in the centre of this picture. The spire of the Welsh church was demolished in the 1950's. Quite a change from today's hectic scene, 4.55 p.m. would not find the Horsefair this quiet! York Publishing Co.

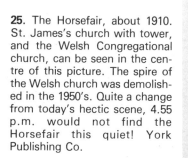

26. Stokes Croft, on a circa-1920 postcard. Prominent in the picture is a large advertisement for Douglas Motors with a combination standing at the pavement. Tram 100 wends its leisurely way to the Horsefair, and Clements the tailors can be seen on the corner of City Road. Most buildings on the left remain, but trade under different names. "Chatterton Series" postcard by A.G. Short and Co.

27. General Hospital, on a card dated August 1917. Wounded soldiers can be seen on the verandahs of the new wing of the old hospital, now little changed in appearance and still in constant use. The original building was designed by William Bruce Gingell, begun in 1852 and completed in 1857.

28. Another view of the General Hospital, looking toward what was the Nurses Home. An early motorised St. John's Ambulance can be seen on the left of the picture, and the fountain in the centre was donated by Joseph Storrs Fry.

29. Y.M.C.A. Dug-out, opened on 17th May, 1917 for the benefit of servicemen. The headquarters of the Y.M.C.A. was later built on this site, but is no longer used by them. Postcard by Burgess and Bown.

30. The Coliseum, originally opened for roller skaters. A different view is shown in book 1, illus. 174. Harvey Barton card.

31. Interior of Coliseum being used as a roller skating rink. This building was also used as a dance hall, ice skating rink, exhibition centre, and the building of aeroplanes during the 1914-1918 war. This part was destroyed in 1940. A "temporary" building (now 35 years old!), stands on part of this site. The postcard, by Harvey Barton, was posted in December 1910.

32. The Art Gallery, looking toward Park Row and Park Street, from Queen's Road, with drinking fountain and horse trough to the right of the picture, both very necessary after toiling up Park Street! No University tower as yet, but the frontage of Blind School can just be seen below the Art Gallery. A Harvey Barton postcard.

33. St. Raphael's church and Almshouses, damaged in the 1939-45 war, and demolished in 1950. Coal trains still travel along this quay to the coal depot at the rear of the Industrial Museum.

34. Vauxhall Bridge, Cumberland Road, with rail track in foreground leading to the goods yard in the picture above. Houses are now being built on the site of the timber yards on the left. A horse and cart belonging to J.S. Fry, the chocolate manufacturers, can be seen, the middle one of three in the centre of the picture.

35. Coronation Road: this postcard shows the opposite side of the Vauxhall Bridge (seen in the card above). Masts of ships in the city dock can be seen on the left of the picture.

36. Redcliffe Wharf, on a picture taken from about the site of Redcliffe Bridge. W.C.A. Mills building still stands, although in a very derelict condition. The barge in the foreground from Avonmouth can be seen unloading grain into the Granary. Published by Etches and Co., Bristol.

37. One of a series of cards issued by the Port of Bristol for the British Empire Exhibition, 1924-25. The view is looking towards St. Augustine's Bridge. About half the waterway in the centre of this picture is now covered. The Bush warehouse, to the right foreground, is now the Arnolfini Gallery.

38. A group of ship-workers from the Albion Dockyard, 26th January, 1918. This was once Hill's shipyards, now a boatyard and marina, although a dry-dock still remains. Photo by E.C. Stevens of Arley Hill.

39. Bristol Grammar School was a very attractive building, situated opposite University College. It was founded in 1532 when Robert Thorne the younger took over the near-destitute St. Bartholomew's Hospital, and was housed in these tiny buildings until the 18th century. The postcard is from a painting by Fritz von Kömptz and published by Raphael Tuck in their 'oilette' series on Clifton.

40. Cheltenham Road in the 1900's with Arley Chapel in the middle distance. The gardens on the left were partially removed for road widening, and later a Cinema was built, centre left. It had several names, the last being the "Academy", which closed in 1955. The building is now used by the Christadelphians.

41. Coldharbour Road (formerly called Coldharbour Lane), leading to Coldharbour Farm on Ashmead's Map of 1882. The road was developed and houses built in 1904. This card, posted in 1905, was published by Wilkinson of Trowbridge.

42. White Hart Inn, Jacobs Wells Road. This old inn was demolished in 1877 to make way for St. Peters church in 1882, which in its turn was demolished in 1939. It was not until 1950 that St. Peters flats were built, thus perpetuating the name.

43. The Old Lime Kiln Dock, Hotwells Road. This was demolished and filled in during 1903, prior to the construction of the railway to the new goods depot at Cannon's Marsh.

LIMEKILN DOCK, BRISTOL.—Built 1626, demolished 1903.   [Copyright by T. C. Pearse.

Hotwells Road, Bristol.

44. Hotwells Road. This was once Love Street, looking to the City end from Dowry Square. Many buildings were demolished for road widening in the 1930's. Tram 228 is travelling to Brislington from Hotwells. Card published by H. Evans, of Hotwells Rd., and posted in September 1907.

45. Ashton Gate, about 1910, on a postcard by A.G. Short and Co. North Street is off to the right, with Coronation Road to the left. The old turnpike building in the centre of the picture is now incorporated into an elderly peoples' dwelling.

Ashton Bridge.

46. Ashton Swing Bridge, on a card postally used in 1910. Railway lines were carried beneath the roadway of this bridge. The picture shows the signal device for shipping using the docks. In the 1950's, when ships no longer used the cut, the bridge was fixed and the control cabin removed. After the completion of the new Cumberland Basin road scheme in the 1970's, the road section was removed, leaving the railway lines exposed. The postcard is in W.H. Smith's "Grosvenor" series.

47. Clifton Suspension Bridge. The picture is taken from the approach road leading to the Swing Bridge. The large white house on the left was the "New Inn", and the tobacco bond warehouses are on the right; note the Rownham ferryman plying his trade in the centre. Postcard by Hepworth.

48. Tower Hill, looking towards Old Market in 1924 shows a flourishing thoroughfare. Bristol Ambulance Station is now on the left and Castlegate, a new office, on the right, all the shops and the public house having been pulled down. Card published by A.G. Roberts of Eastville.

49. Old Market Street in 1939, with the tower of the Central Hall middle right, and in centre distance Castle Street. Photograph by John W. Garratt who took many fine views of Bristol spanning the decades.

50. Celebrations for the visit of King George V and Queen Mary to Bristol. Brick Street near Trinity Road Police Station in St. Philips is now pulled down. But what a community spirit existed then!

HENBURY AND WESTBURY

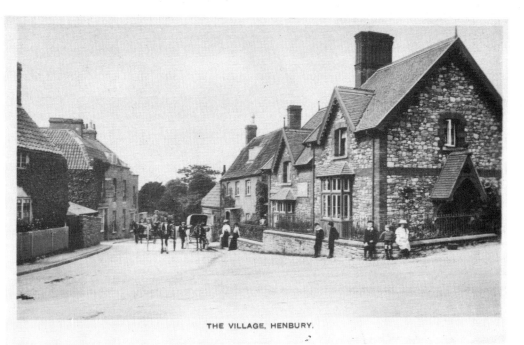

THE VILLAGE, HENBURY.

51. This view of Henbury is looking from the main entrance of Blaise Castle Estate, with Blaise Inn on the left and the road on the right leading to the Church. The road is now a one way system, but still retains its village atmosphere.

Blaise Castle House. 877. Bristol.

52. Blaise Castle House, owned by the Harfords family, and bought for the citizens of Bristol in 1926. This view, postally used in 1936, shows the stone balustrade around the house intact. The balustrade was damaged during the 1939-45 war when used by military personnel. Photo by J.W. Garratt.

53. This view has not changed much, the "White Lion" still flourishing. The turning (right) leads to the oldest part of Westbury and Dial House. The river Trym flows underground at this point from Badock Woods, in Southmead. Postcard by Harvey Barton.

High St & Passage Rd. Westbury.

SEA MILLS AND SHIREHAMPTON

54. Sea Mills was developed as a housing estate at the same time as Knowle, between 1925-30. It was particularly attractively laid out with trees and grass verges. Postally used in 1928.

55. Sea Mills square in 1938. Note the early bus and telephone kiosk, and Kingsweston Woods in the distance. Message on the back of the postcard: *"Just moved here, what a pleasant place it is!"*

56. Sylvan Way is one of the longest roads in Sea Mills. It begins at Coombe Dingle and finishes at the Portway. This card was posted in 1935.

57. The small house on the left was the former lodge to Shirehampton Park Estate, which is still to be seen today. The hill leads down into Shirehampton Village, now a much wider thoroughfare. Postally used 1918, and published by S.E. Robinson, Post Office, Shirehampton.

58. High Street, Shirehampton, in 1909, with the Old Manor House just showing in the middle distance. That has gone but the rest of the street is unchanged but for some modernisation to shop fronts. There is still the tree in front of the Wesleyan Church, and note the fine lamp on the right.

59. This view looks up towards Shirehampton Village, with the centre distance now a busy traffic light junction. Published locally by E.S. Pearce, Post Office, Shirehampton.

Royal Edward Warehouse. (showing centre railroad hauling ways)

60. Another Port of Bristol card issued for the Empire Exhibition, showing the warehouse where goods were brought from ships in the dock by rail to await delivery by rail or road.

Swing Bridge. Avonmouth Docks. 434.

61. Swing Bridge, Avonmouth. This bridge spans the junction between Avonmouth old dock on the left and the Royal Edward dock on the right. Postally used 1921.

62. Continental Hotel, originally called the Avonmouth Hotel, and opened in April 1865. It was situated in the Pleasure Gardens, with a concert hall and ornamental lake, very near the station of the Port and Pier railway. The first excursion to the Pleasure Gardens ran on 11th July, 1866. The hotel was taken over by the City Corporation in 1902 and used as a residence for the chief engineer in charge of the building of the Royal Edward Dock. It became a collecting centre for emigrants from the Continent, awaiting passage to U.S.A. and Canada. This was when it became the "Continental" hotel. Taken over by the army during the 1914-18 war, it was demolished in 1926.

63. Victoria Street, Clifton, now Princess Victoria Street; looking toward Regent Street, with the Mall off left. The architecture has changed very little, though the building foreground left is now a restaurant. This is a very popular shopping area, and the roadway is often congested.

64. St. Michael's Hill, on a watercolour by Evacustes Phipson, published by J. Salmon. One of the first streets built out of the old city in the late 17th century when merchants wanted to live away from the smells of a crowded city - up on the hill there was fresh air!

65. Broad Weir, by Evacustes Phipson. Taylors the printers occupied the gabled 16th-century building, destroyed in the air raid of 28th August, 1942. Next door is the "Crown" Inn, which was demolished in the 1960's, and Philadelphia Street can be seen off to the right. This was a notorious street, known to older Bristolians as Philly-i-fy Street.

BISHOPSWORTH

Post Office, Bishopsworth.

66. Bishopsworth in the 1930's. Church Road is off to the right, with Whitchurch Road left leading to Hartcliffe and the new Wills complex. All the buildings have gone, to be replaced by swimming baths and shops.

67. Bishopsworth, a tranquil scene now transformed into a housing estate. Kings Head Lane is off to the right at the bottom of the hill. The card was postally used in 1912.

68. Bishopsworth, the village. The opposite view to the above, looking towards the city. The buildings on the right have been demolished and a new Post Office built and the road widened.

KNOWLE AND TOTTERDOWN

Bath & Wells Road, Bristol.

69. Three Lamps, on a postcard used in 1911. All the buildings were demolished in 1972-73 for a controversial road scheme, but the famous 3-lamps sign post, showing Bath to the left and Wells to the right, has recently been restored to approximately its original position. Smiths, the undertakers, can be seen to the left of the picture, having their roof attended to, with a shaving saloon near the tram wire stanchion. Small businesses on the central corner include a watchmaker, steam laundry, and house agent.

70. Wells Road, Knowle. Tram route no. 10 on its way from Knowle to Bristol Bridge. A quiet scene, so different from today's bustle, and the trees no longer need their metal frames. Posted in 1920. An A.G. Short and Co. postcard.

Wells Road, Knowle, Bristol.

The Tennis Courts, Knowle.

71. The Tennis Courts, Knowle. The houses seen in the background are in Wells Road. Priory Road is behind the pavilion, and the photograph was taken before Broad Walk came into being, taking part of the tennis courts. Note the dress of the lady in the foreground, and the shape of her tennis racquet. Postcard by Harvey Barton.

BRISLINGTON

Old Brislington, Bristol.

72. Old Brislington, with H.C. Windmill, saddler and harness-maker on the far corner opposite Bridge House refreshment rooms. The Post Office was originally Albert House, the home of N.J. West, carpenter and undertaker. The smithy can be seen left foreground, with a milk cart parked outside. Where the ash tree is in the picture, there was a yard with a stone platform for re-tyring carriage and cart wheels. Card posted in 1912.

School Road, Brislington, Bristol.

73. School Road, about 1922. This is virtually the same now, except that the cottages front left of picture, School Place, have been demolished. Above the wall on the right was St. Lukes church school. A.G. Short and Company published the card.

74. West Town Lane, a view looking toward the Bath Road. The stream to the left flows to Water Lane. Postcard by L.T. Elson of Sandy Park Road, Brislington.

The Old Bridge, West Town Lane, Brislington.

75. St. Anne's School, built before 1902. This school is still in use today, and stands on the corner of Bloomfield Road and Langton Court Road. A delightful group of children is posing outside with a teacher. Note the little boy climbing the lamp-post!

76. Brooklea, about 1905, once the home, in 1900, of A.J. Smith, who became Lord Mayor 1905-7. His grandson, Alfred Parry, was a well-known historian of Brislington. The U.S. Army occupied the house in 1943, and it was demolished in 1950, but Brooklea health centre perpetuates the name today. A wonderful array of hats is worn by the ladies and gentlemen.

77. Salisbury Road. St. Anne's church on the left was consecrated on 3rd October 1909. The fenced land on the right was acquired by St. Anne's parish hall trustees in October 1913 for a church hall, and a temporary building was opened in June 1921 by Alderman Britton at a cost of £1,700. Card posted in 1910.

HANHAM

78. Pound Ebenezer Sunday School, opened in 1880, was pulled down for road widening in 1962. Hanham Methodist Chapel on the right has been replaced by modern premises, and is still flourishing. The card was published by S. Burgess, Post Office, Hanham.

79. A view of Hanham High Street just further along from the Pound. The 199 tram is on the route between Old Market St. and Hanham.

80. This postcard shows the centre of Hanham village in 1905. The house on the right with the porch was the Police Station, and is now a private house, with the porch removed. Shops stand today in the centre of the picture, and the building on the left is privately owned, though formerly occupied by the Anchor Boot Company, and later Lloyds Bank. The area behind the tram is now being developed with new houses. "Avonvale series" postcard by J.B. and S.C., posted in Bristol in August 1905.

78. Hanham, Bristol.

81. Beaufort War Hospital was used for casualties of the 1914-18 war. This view of the laundry shows good guard protection from the roller machines. It is now Glenside Hospital, and externally not changed a great deal. A Viner postcard.

82. Looking from Fishponds Road, known as the "straits", with Fishponds Park and the spire of St. Mary's Church in the distance. The card was postally used in 1916, and published by Viner and Co.

83. Fishponds Road looking towards the "Full Moon" Hotel. Fishponds was originally known as 'New Pools', so-called because in the 12th century there were Monks' pools on the site of the present Post Office adjoining the "Full Moon" Hotel. Electric trams reached this area in 1897, and, within a few months, Staple Hill. A Garratt card.

84. Stapleton Road, built in the peak of Victorian development, showing solid architecture, and still a shopping area today. It is the beginning of a thoroughfare, starting in Easton on this view and continuing to the bottom of Bell Hill, Stapleton.

85. This postcard is where the main South Wales line crosses Stapleton Road at Eastville, also used by the one local line still in use to Avonmouth and Severn Beach.

The shops on the right have either been demolished or are in a very run-down condition. Illus. 77 in volume one looks in the opposite direction. Postcard by Hepworth, postally used in 1925.

86. A close-up view of the former tram terminus at Eastville, showing the Methodist Church (compare illus. 78, volume one). This postcard clearly shows Stapleton Road as it wends left towards Bristol Rovers' football ground. The M32 now extends across the middle distance, and the church was demolished many years ago.

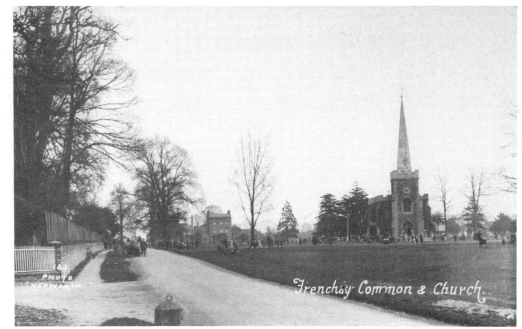

87. Frenchay Common still retains its village atmosphere, in spite of development. On the left, Cedar Hall and grounds are incorporated in Frenchay Hospital, which borders the left hand side of the Common; many of the trees still survive. Postcard by Hepworth.

88. The Turnpike House stood at the junction of Stapleton Road and Glenfrome Road, by Stapleton Bridge, and was in use until 1867 as a Toll House. It was finally pulled down for road widening in 1929. The Railway Viaduct used to span Stapleton Road.

89. Stapleton Bridge at the bottom of Bell Hill, where it spans the River Frome, was in use until 1929, when it was replaced by a wider bridge. There were further alterations when the M.32 motorway was constructed. The elevated section runs above Muller Road, towards central Bristol, above this junction.

DOWNEND

90. Downend, as shown on this postcard, is completely changed; only the memorial to Boy Scouts and part of the "Horseshoe Inn" remain, though the latter has been enlarged and modernised. This view by Hepworth was postally used in 1926. The bus has a Gloucestershire registration number.

91. Downend Road has changed very little since 1926 when this photograph was taken, but how much quieter it is compared with the bustling traffic of today! A Hepworth postcard.

92. This is a 1950's view of the centre of Downend. Compare with the earlier view on this page. The "Horseshoe Inn" on the right, and the Boy Scout monument can be seen in front of the 'Fine Fare' store. Card published by Harvey Barton and Son Ltd.

93. Gloucester Road, Bishopston on the corner of Nevil Road. The corner shop is still a chemist, but decoration on the twin towers of Horfield Baptist Church has been removed. Postally used in 1907.

94. Looking up Gloucester Road towards "Pigstye Hill", mentioned on illus. 97. Sommerville Road is on the right, and today a garage stands on the left of the picture, with shops on the right. One of the boys is in Scout uniform.

FOUNDATION STONE-LAYING-PARISH HALL BISHOPSTON.

95. The foundation stone for Bishopston Church Halls, of St. Michaels and All Angels Church, was laid on September 11th 1907 by Mrs. G.A. Gibbs. These halls, which consisted of several adjoining rooms, were attached to the older Church of England School room. Several halls have been demolished in recent years to make way for accommodation for elderly people. A Garratt postcard.

96. This road in Bishopston leads to Gloucester Road, and the Methodist Church can just be seen. The road is little changed today, but the charming group of children help to capture it as it was in 1905. The postcard was published by Kelly and Harvey of Gloucester Rd.

97. This view of Gloucester Road called locally "Pigstye Hill", is unchanged since this card was published, apart from the removal of tram lines. St. Matthew's Church, Kingsdown, can be seen on the skyline.

98. This Bishopston group outing before 1910 features the Blaise Castle folly in the background, in the days when it was a private estate belonging to the Harfords. Photographic postcard by J.W. Garratt of Ashley Down.

99. Ashley Hill Station Hotel, pre-1910, situated across the bridge in illus. 101. Gentlemen pose before entering the hostelry while the ladies take the baby for a walk across the fields. Colman's Special Scotch is advertised on the hotel window.

100. The "Shakespeare Express". A Great Western Railway locomotive, 'County' class, with a head of steam, heading towards Filton. Card posted in 1913.

101. Girls from the Mullers Orphanage, in their distinctive uniform "off for their annual outing". The large building on the skyline from the left to centre is the orphanage, which was built in 1862. The card was posted in September 1921.

HORFIELD

102. Horfield Barracks, used as a depot by the Gloucestershire Regt., was built between 1845-47; only the outside retaining wall now remains. New offices were built in the grounds in the 1960's. Viners published the card, which was postally used in 1921.

103. Horfield Church of England School before the construction of Kellaway Avenue and Wellington Hill. The school is now closed and used for Youth Activities. Postcard by Garratt.

104. Kellaway Avenue was opened in 1921, and named after the then Postmaster General, F.G. Kellaway M.P. This view by Garratt is looking towards Gloucester Road North. The farm on the left is gone and new houses have been built.

105. Bedminster Parade, from Regent Road looking toward Bedminster Bridge. The "new" Police Station - built 1882 and now obsolete - can be seen on the left, with the castle frontage. Close by is the Bristol Free Library, c.1900.

106. New Library, Bedminster. Photograph taken in the early 1920's. This replaced the Free Library seen in the picture above. The Temperance Hall, originally on this site, was demolished in 1913. The old Free Library was replaced by the Bedminster Picture Drome, showing silent films.

107. Victoria Park, with Totterdown to the left and as yet no Perretts Park or houses spreading to Knowle. The swimming baths in the foreground were used as an emergency water supply during World War 2, and then they were demolished. Postcard by H.B. & S. Ltd., postally used in June 1912.

CLIFTON

108. The Observatory was originally a windmill, which burnt down in 1777. The tower was restored and contains a camera obscura with fine views of the surrounding area. There is also an underground passage leading to Ghyston Cave, overlooking the Avon Gorge. Published by Viners of Bath.

109 Clifton Down Hotel, opened in 1865. This view, taken from a road leading from the Suspension Bridge, shows early fashion and transport, about 1915.

110. This charming group was taken in Royal York Crescent, Clifton. The message on the back of the postcard reads: *"Happy recollections of the Motor rides at Clifton, September 1905".*

Whiteladies Gate, Clifton.

H. B. & S.

111. Whiteladies Gate in 1905. The cab stand and cabman's hut serving Clifton Down station have now gone. Today a modern shopping complex adjoins the station. Harvey Barton postcard.

112. The fountain which was built as a memorial to Rev. Urijah Thomas in 1903. He was minister at Redland Park Congregational Church and was remembered for his charity work. Posted in 1904.

113. The tram terminus at Belgrave Road, with Blackboy Hill on the left. The tank, from the 1914-18 war, was on display to advertise War Bond savings. The houses in the background are little changed. Photographic postcard no. 452 in A.G.S. & Co's "Chatterton series".

Belgrave Rd. Durdham Downs, Bristol.

A.G.S.&Co 452.

Tramway Company's Electric Power Station, BRISTOL.
No. 184.   THE "PROGRESS" SERIES.   T. H. S. & CO.   B. & C.

114. Tram 29, route 3, travelling between Durdham Downs and Eastville. It was built in 1900 by the Midland Railway Carriage and Wagon Company Ltd., of Birmingham. Photographed in Redland in October 1919, when young ladies were employed as "clippies". The driver is Frederick Houghton, a Barton Hill man, who died on 5th February, 1977.

115. Electric Power Station. Originally a chapel, then it became a sugar refinery. Bristol Tramways and Carriage Co. Ltd rebuilt and enlarged the premises in the late 1890's. Situated by the river at St. Philips Bridge, it was in an ideal position for the supply of coal by barge. When the bridge was hit by a bomb in 1941, it severed the supply of electricity to the remaining tram services. The building is now part of Courage's brewery.

116. Tram 124 at the top of Blackboy Hill, on the Durdham Down to Zetland Road route. The trolley is on one of the reversers at Durdham Down Terminus. Tram 236 approaches from Westbury Road Junction.

DECORATED TRAMS

Bristol Tramways Illuminated Car. December 1922.

117-9. The decorated trams of the 1920's were always popular, besides supporting a very worthwhile cause. The 1923 tram is always referred to as the "Christmas Pudding" for obvious reasons. One or two facts which readers may find interesting: the 1922 tram had approximately 525 lights and raised £1,171. The 1923 tram had approximately 706 lights and the total of £1,212 was raised. Quite incredible sums! All the photographs were taken at Brislington depot.

Bristol Tramways. Illuminated Car. December 1923.

Bristol Tramways Illuminated Tram. December, 1926.

FIRE BRIGADE

120. The horse-drawn Fire Engine, as in use in 1882. This postcard was by Fred Little.

Bristol Police Fire Brigade 1906.

121. Bristol Police Fire Brigade at the rear of the old Bridewell, with two turntable ladders, and engine run by steam. The jackets have the double row of buttons, similar to present day uniforms. Photo by F. Snary, Castle Street, 1906.

122. The yearly inspection of the Bristol Fire Brigade in July 1932, outside the new Bridewell. The gentleman in civilian clothes is Superintendant Cade. Card published by Veale and Co., Bristol.

123. Bristol City A.F.C. This 1932-3 team was virtually a new line-up, with only four key players remaining from the previous season, because of their desperate financial position. They finished at the bottom of the second division the previous season, and it was about this time that the City appointed a new manager, Bob Hewison, the gentleman in the light jacket, and he remained with the club for 16 years. The above photograph shows the players in front of No. 1 ground stand which was destroyed by incendiary bombs during the second world war.

Copyright. **BRISTOL ROVERS FOOTBALL TEAM.—Season 1904-5.**

G. W. PAY, *Trainer* WILSON PUDAN CARTLIDGE DUNN CLARK (D.) WASSELL A. G. HOMER, *Secretary*
G. W. HUMPHREYS, *Chairman* HALES JARVIE APPLEBY GRIFFITHS DUNKLEY S. S. RINDER, *Vice-Chairman*
SMITH CLARK (W.) BEATS, *Captain* LEWIS TAIT

124. Bristol Rovers Football team, 1904-5. Bristol's other football team - soccer really was a serious business in 1904!

SCHOOLS

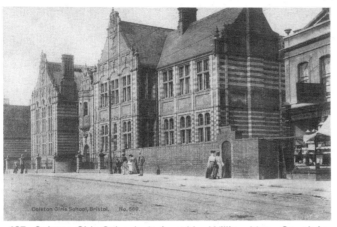

125. Colston Girls School, designed by William Venn Gough in 1891. The building incorporates a variety of styles but is very attractive. It has recently been extended in a manner sympathetic to the original.

126. Kingswood School, on a card posted in 1905. The school is still used and situated in the High Street, which is far more congested today! A Midland Railway wagon wends its way up the hill.

127. City School, known as Queen Elizabeth's Hospital School, a boarding school for boys, with a very distinctive uniform. The architects of this elegant castellated building were Thomas Foster & Son, 1844-7.

128. St. George Higher Grade School, opened on 15th November 1894. It was the first of its kind in the West of England, and was run by the St. George School Board, fees being 5d a week. The first headmaster was Mr. F.W. Westaway, and Mr. Frederick Pickles was in charge from April 1895 until 1929. A Victorian iron toilet can be seen near the horse and cart, close to the two houses and forge. These last have now been replaced by flower beds.

129. A group of pupils outside St. George school, about 1915. The two wooden doors have now been replaced by glass ones. The master at right of the group is believed to be Mr. Halliwell.

130. St. Mary's on the Quay. This building stood in Trenchard Street opposite the back of the Colston Hall. Fresh air and exercise were definitely the order of the day!

131. Stapleton Road Station, on the Bristol-South Wales via New Passage ferry line, was opened on 8th September 1863. The station nameboard proclaims "Stapleton Road Junction for South Wales and Avonmouth". A superb real photographic postcard with plenty of animation: a good complement of porters and passengers. Posted at Bristol in September 1907.

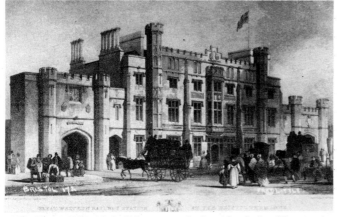

132. Situated in this building were the booking hall, offices and board room of the G.W.R. Company, whose Paddington to Bristol line opened in June 1841, designed by Isambard Kingdom Brunel. A Fred Little photo.

133. This is the original Great Western station, also designed by I.K.B. and the oldest in the world, now thankfully being restored after being used as a car park. An exhibition inside this building to mark the 150th anniversary of the Great Western Railway was opened by the Queen in July 1985.

134. A picture of no. 2 platform at Temple Meads station. A "write-in" card by local publisher Barnett of North Street, and postally used in 1904. The mention of St. Philips refers to the terminus of the Midland railway in Midland road.

135. Patchway Station. A picture of the second station of 1885, replacing the one built in 1863. Originally named Patchway and Stoke Gifford, it was renamed Patchway on 27th October, 1908. The postcard was published by A. Emery of the Post Office, Patchway, and sent from Bristol in October 1907.

136. Clifton Bridge Station, set in very attractive surroundings. Opened on 18th April, 1867, on the Bristol to Portishead railway. The name was changed to Rownham station in 1891. The line was closed to passenger traffic on 7th September 1964, but was re-opened for excursions to celebrate the 150th anniversary of the Great Western Railway. No publisher mentioned on the card.

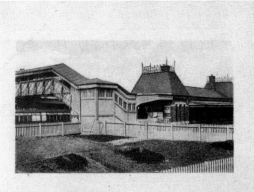

137. Bedminster Railway Station. This elegant building was originally owned by the Bristol and Exeter Railway in 1870, and at that time there were only two lines. It was rebuilt in the early 1930's, when the track was widened to four lines. Card published by C.S. and Co.

138. Pear Stone and tunnel,'St. Anne's Park. The no. 2 tunnel out of Temple Meads. The Pear Stone is reputed to have been dug out when the tunnel was constructed. The view is looking toward Bath, and the card was posted in 1905.

139. St. Anne's station, on a card posted in 1909. The photograph was taken from the top of Nightingale Valley. This station was opened on May 23rd 1898, on the Bristol to Bath Great Western line, and was one of the few in the area which never dealt with goods traffic. The grassy bank is now largely covered with bungalows.

SHOPS

140. Pleasance & Harper. The frontage of the Jewellers' at 4, Wine Street. Stuckey's Restaurant is to the right of the picture. Later it was to become J. Lyons.

141. Milsom & Son, Park Street, renowned suppliers of pianos and supporter of the Bristol Eisteddfod, a £50 piano being given by them in 1905 to Vivian Languish. In 1923 John Bennett, jeweller, moved to 82 Park Street, from College Green. This is now the premises of the Speedy Photo Service.

142. Messrs. Woolway of Stokes Croft, between City Road and Ashley Road. A wonderful array of gents' apparel! This firm is no longer in existence.

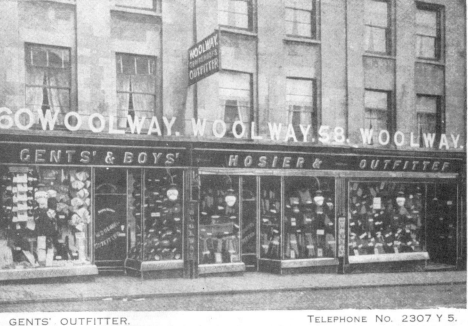

143. James Phillips. This photo was taken at Whiteladies Road. The firm was founded in 1800, but has now gone out of business, and new shops are trading where the head office used to be in Union Street. A shoeing forge can be seen to the left of the picture.

144. The Durdham Down cafe, on Blackboy Hill, next to Gyles Sports shop, which is still trading. The picture was taken around the 1920's. Saphire Productions now occupy no. 184, whilst Raybrake and Co., motor factors, are at 186.

145. High Street, about 1910. All these shops stood between the entrance to the flower market and St. Nicholas Street, but were destroyed in the 1940 air-raids. The shop on the right is the Public Benefit Boot Company.

CHARACTERS

146. What a wonderful face! Coat done up with large safety pins, a straw hat, and a feather boa. Bedminster Biddy in all her glory!

147. Paper Sally. One of the real old characters of Bristol, who sold papers around the central area in the late 1800's and early this century, until she died of suffocation in a fire on Christmas Day 1926, in her paper-filled rooms on the first floor of 2 Deep Street, St. James. She was given a funeral by the Police of "A" division as a final tribute.

148. Bristol's Town Crier. Joseph Croot, Bristol's last "Crier", was appointed to the ancient office in 1855, though it lapsed about 1891. Mr. Croot lived in Goodhind Street, where he died in 1899 and was buried in Downend churchyard. The brass buttons on his coat bore the Bristol Coat of Arms and he always wore a bunch of flowers attached to his coat.

ROYAL VISITS

149. Clare Street decorated for the Royal visit of 1908, when King Edward VII and Queen Alexandra came to open the Royal Edward dock at Avonmouth.

150. Marlborough Street, June 18th, 1912. King George V and Queen Mary arriving at the Royal Infirmary for the official opening of this memorial to King Edward VII. A photographer in a bowler hat can be seen just above the canopy to the right of the picture. Card published by A.G. Short & Co.

151. The arrival of the King and Queen at Temple Meads station on 28th June, 1912. Superb decorations and guard of honour.

BRISTOL ZOO

152. The Pelicans. York Publishing Co. Bristol, card no. **1886.** The message on the back of the card is very interesting:-
"Funny birds these, they have a larder under their chin. Tommy saw them arriving in a milk cart!"

153. Zoological Gardens, on a postcard published by Viner, Bath. This attractive building was replaced by a cafeteria in the 1930's. Postally used in 1916.

154. 1930's photograph by F.L. Vanderplank of children enjoying a ride on 'Judy'. The Zoo gardens are still beautiful and attract many visitors each year.

155. Though not published as an advertising card, this superb photographic postcard would serve the same purpose as far as William Gale was concerned! This firm of bakers and confectioners traded in Whiteladies Road from 1906 to 1940. The handcart was a popular form of delivery into the 1940's.

156. Georges Brewery was founded in 1788 - in the 1870's it was to be found at the Old Porter Brewery, Bath Street. The old farmer in the picture certainly seems to be enjoying his home-brewed!

ADVERT CARDS

157. Royal Hotel. An elegant Victorian hotel, once the headquarters of the Royal Automobile Club. Now alas empty, awaiting redevelopment.

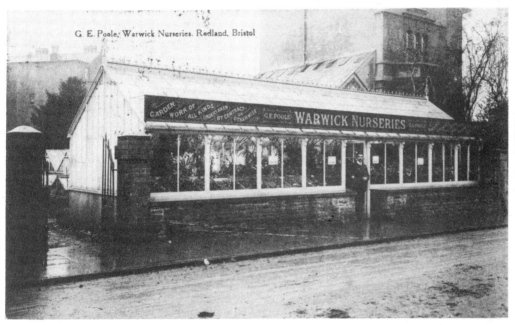

158. Mr. Poole's nurseries in Warwick Road, Redland. The postcard was sent by G.E. Poole himself, thanking a Mr. Tedder of Westbury-on-Trym for his advice, and posted in February 1907.

159. "George & Railway" Hotel. This establishment is still in business, but not in a very quiet position, with the amount of traffic which passes the building constantly. A statue of Queen Victoria is just visible on the right. The proprietor named on this pre-1918 card is Mrs. Nation.

160. Fishponds Pottery. Bristol has been known for its excellent pottery since 1652. Shown here is the factory of Pountneys Bristol Pottery.

161. Trent pottery loving cup, showing the Bristol Coat of Arms. Postcard by Trent Bridge Publishing Co., Stoke-on-Trent, and postally used in 1906.

162. White Hart Hotel. A very busy scene on Brislington Hill. Thursday being market day, it seems the owner of the cart standing outside the hostelry has decided on some refreshment before continuing his journey home. Could the covered wagon be a furniture removal cart? Linden Farm, centre picture, supplied most of the village from its dairy, and was demolished in 1924 for houses.

163. A rare advertising card produced by locomotive engineers Peckett & Sons Ltd. The reverse is used as an acknowledgement of receipt of an order for locomotive parts from Manchester Corporation. In 1880 Peckett & Sons took over the business established by Fox Walker & Co. at the Atlas Engine Works, St. George, Bristol. Four members of the Peckett family were associated with the firm, Wilfred and Roy remaining until the business was taken over by Reed Crane & Hoist Co. Ltd. on 23rd October, 1961.

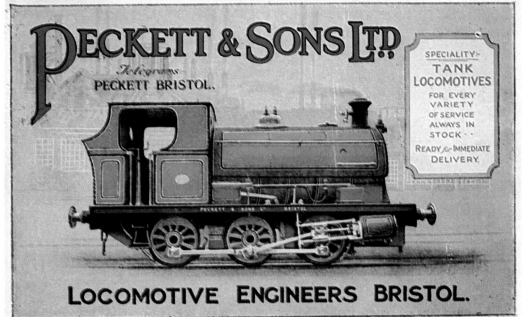

164. Can this be a sideline of two of our compilers? They certainly cover a wide range of travelling gear!

165. Blotter and advertisement, published by E.W. Savory Ltd., Bristol. Rather an apt quotation for a business firm.

A LAST GLIMPSE OF BRISTOL

166. Historic King Street , the home of the oldest theatre in England, the Theatre Royal, and also the Llandoger Trow, which is reputed to be the inn mentioned in *Treasure Island*. An appealing group of children in the foreground display interest in the photographer. Carter and horse have evidently gone for refreshment!

167. The "Hatchet Inn", Frogmore Street, was once a 16th century farmhouse, which became an inn in 1606. Isolated on an island near the 'Mecca' entertainment centre, it has recently been renovated and re-named 'A.D. 1606'.

168. Clare Street and Baldwin Street, showing the well-known Glass's Corner. The Sun Insurance building also houses Walker & Hall, Ltd., silversmiths. The Clare Street Picture house can be seen in the bottom left hand corner. On the bill was Mary Pickford. Card posted in 1917.

AERIAL VIEWS

169. Temple Meads Station. This photograph and the two plates following are all aerial views published by Photochrom Co. Ltd., London, by arrangement with the Aircraft Manufacturing Co. Ltd. This picture was taken before the alterations to the station in 1932. Note the engine shed to the right of the picture; this was situated in Cattle Market Road. The kiln of the Phoenix glass works can be seen just off centre.

170. Queen Square, before it was desecrated by a dual carriageway! The tall chimneys of J.S. Fry & Son, chocolate manufacturers, can be seen to the top left of the picture.

171. Redcliffe Hill in all its glory! Shot tower can be seen opposite St. Mary Redcliffe spire. Most of the buildings in the foreground have been replaced by blocks of offices and flats.

LOCAL POSTCARD PUBLISHERS

Most of the publishers of Bristol postcards were small firms or sub-postmasters, catering for a very limited demand. Only a few, for example E.W. Savory, Charles Worcester, and Harvey Barton, published material of non-local interest. Much research needs to be done on most of these concerns to determine the scope of their output, and the compilers would be pleased to receive any further information about them, and indeed about any hitherto undiscovered postcard publishers. An * indicates that cards by a particular publisher feature in the book.

Art Printers Ltd.
*J. Baker & Son, The Mall, Clifton
*R. Barnett, North Street
*Harvey Barton & Son Ltd. (H.B. & S.)
J.A. Bickle, Whiteladies Gate
Blyth
W. Brisley, Park Street
Brown & Lloyd, Portland Place, Clifton
*S. Burgess, Post Office, Hanham
*Burgess & Bown
*Burgess & Co., "Bee" series
Burleigh Ltd.
Castle Stationery Co.
Chappell & Co., Redcliffe Printing Works
M.L. Chubb, Shirehampton Post Office
E. Coe, St. Annes Post Office
A.E. Comer, Brislington
F.O. Coward, Bedminster
"Dodson" series
H. Edbrooke, Clifton
*L.T. Elson, Brislington & Bristol
*A. Emery, Post Office, Patchway
*Etches & Co.
*H. Evans, Hotwells Road
A.W. Ford
*W. Garratt, 9 Station Rd., Ashley Down
A.E. Giddings, Abbots Leigh Post Office
E.J. Giddings, Mangotsfield
Gray & Farr, 35 Abbotsford Road, Redland
H.S. Griffin, 3 Highbury Parade, Bristol
Guillon & Son, Fishponds
J.A. Hamilton, Staple Hill
Hardings, "Progress" series
Haywards, 1 Corn Street & 49 High Street
*Hepworth, 66 Church Road, Horfield
W. Hepworth, 366 Gloucester Road
W.M. Hill, 19 Chelsea Park
Henry Hodder & Co. Ltd., Pioneer Cash Chemists
A. Hodgson, 64 Victoria Street
E.C. Hollister, Sandy Park Post Office
A.E. Hornsey, Bedminster Parade
Horton
*J.B. & S.C., "Avonvale" series
*Kelly & Harvey, Gloucester Road

*Fred Little (reproduction of Victorian photographs)
Wilfrid Loft, 323 Wells Road, Knowle
S. Loxton, 7 St. Augustin's Parade
W.F. Mack, 52 Park Row
A.H.N. Middleton
Mitchell & Co., 30 Baldwin Street
"Ozograph" series, 145 St. Michaels Hill
D.G. Parker, 4 Birchwood Road, St. Annes Park
*E.S. Pearce, Post Office Shirehampton
Pincock Bros.
*Plucknett, Kingswood
M.J.R.
Rising, 156 Whitladies Road, Clifton
*A.G. Roberts, Eastville
*S.E. Robinson, Shirehampton Post Office
A.F.S.
*C.S. & Co.
*E.W. Savory & Co.
Scholastic Trading Co.
Senior & Co., Cotham Hill
J.T. Shapland
*A.G. Short & Co, "Chatterton" series
F.C. Sincock, The Library, Westbury-on-Trym
A.E. Smith, 44 College Green
*F. Snary, 26 Castle Street
W.A.W. Sprod, 101 Stokes Croft
T. Stanley, East Street, Bedminster
*E.C. Stevens, 12 Arley Hill
W. Stevenson, Bruton Place, Clifton
Stevinson, "C" series
F.W. Taylor, Clifton
S.J. Thomas, Boyces Avenue, Clifton
*Veale and Co., Bristol
*Viner and Co., Bath and Weston-super-Mare
West Counties Agency, 14 Westfield Park, Redland
Wickhams Ltd.
Winchester
Stanley Wood, Sea Mills Post Office
Charles Worcester & Co.
Wyman & Sons Ltd.
*York Publishing Co.
"York" series, 11 Lower Maudlin Street
*J.C. Young, Redfield

NATIONAL PUBLISHERS

Most of the leading British Picture Postcard Publishers produced views of all the major cities, towns, and tourist resorts. Those who are represented by an illustration in this book are:

Cynicus Publishing Co. Ltd.
Photocrom Co. Ltd.
A.C. Redman & Co., Southsea
J. Salmon Ltd.

W.H. Smith & Son
Trent Bridge Publishing Co.
Raphael Tuck & Sons Ltd.

Valentine's, Dundee
John Walker & Co. Ltd.
R. Wilkinson, Trowbridge

172. Regent Street, Kingswood. Part of the Whitsuntide procession, showing a contingent of the Boys Brigade, possibly from the Kingswood Wesleyan Church, where the captain was Mr. Caddick. This procession of witness is still held every Whitsuntide. The photographer was Plucknett of Kingswood, who took some superb shots of the area.

173. The 5th Gloucester Regiment marching up Corn Street in 1914. The picture is taken from the roof of the Commercial Rooms. Rather an untidy column - probably they were raw recruits, volunteers for Kitchener's army. Corn Street has changed very little over the years, and is still a street of elegant business houses.

174. A novelty 'pull-out' postcard, with a dozen Bristol views on a concertina strip of paper inside the flap. This particular design was published by the Photocrom Co. Ltd. about 1928.

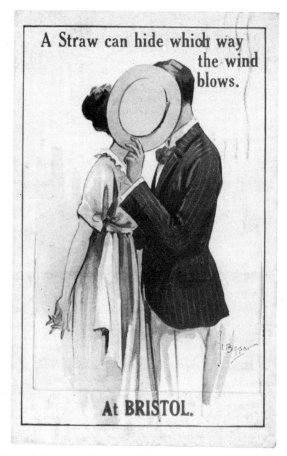

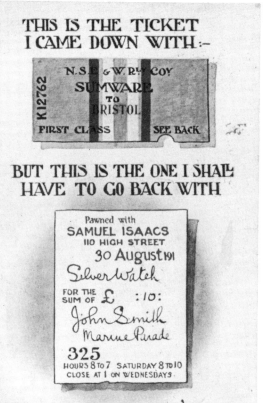

175. A similar novelty card, this time in the E.T.W. Dennis "Dainty" series, and drawn by J.L. Biggar. All these pull-out cards could be overprinted with the name of any desired place, and relevant views included under the flap. This card was sent from Bristol in July 1924.

176. 'Bristol' has been overprinted on the ticket at the top of the postcard, which was published by Joseph Asher & Co. It was sent from Westbury-on-Trym in September 1913, with the message *"Just one more for your collection"*.

SPECIAL PICTURE OFFER

A number of the illustrations in this book are available as enlarged pictures, mounted on green or maroon board in a 12 x 9 inch mount. Each costs £3.50, and they can be obtained direct from the publishers postfree, or ordered from Derek Fisher (Bristol 423177). Pictures available:

1 Broad Quay	83 Fishponds Road	90 Downend
12 Park Street	84 Stapleton Road	93 Gloucester Road, Bishopston
17 Narrow Wine Street	86 Eastville Tram Terminus	100 Shakespeare Express
48 Tower Hill	89 Stapleton Bridge	131 Stapleton Road Station

Mounted pictures are also available of the following locations from illustrations featured in volume 1:

Castle Street; Broad Street; Gloucester Road; Grosvenor Road; Ashley Down; Filton Tram Terminus; Tramways Centre; Bristol Bridge; Blackboy Hill; Old Market Street; Bedminster; Ashley Hill Station; Park Row; St. Andrews Park; Staple Hill.

Just a line from BRISTOL.

177. This comic card speaks for itself! Postally used in 1913 and published by A.C. Redman and Co., Southsea. 'Spithead' series, no. 1504.

178. From the "Cynicus" range. This was the pen-name of Scottish satirical artist Martin Anderson, who formed his own postcard publishing company in Tayport, Fife. The card was used in 1908, but was published about six years earlier. Message is again self-explanatory.

179. The sender of this card seemed not to have much luck either, as she states she is leaving Bristol in January *"to try my luck elsewhere"*. Very intriguing! The Cynicus postcard of the lady giving up hope of finding a husband in Clifton is most appropriate. Posted in December 1908.